I0540047

DANCING
WITH MY
SOUL

A Collection of Poems, Thoughts and Photographs

SARAH CATHERINE SMITH

ISBN: 979-8-89633-002-8 (sc)
ISBN: 979-8-89633-003-5 (e)

Page Solutions - Bluegrass Bound Books
541 Buttermilk Pike
Crescent Springs, KY 41017

Printed in the United States of America

Contents

Dedication

I dedicate this book to my husband, Kevin for his encouragement and love; to the Gardenia Center for their continued support and prayers; to my friend David Duncan who gave me the idea to start writing; to my higher power for allowing me to be a vessel for my poems and finally to my two beautiful daughters Emily and Elizabeth who challenge everyday to be better.

Introduction

I was emotionally and verbally abused all my life. It was a struggle growing up, as I had very low self- esteem and felt rejected. My mother did not know how to love. She grew up in a very strict German household. I was the first, so what my mother knew or did not know was passed on to me. She wanted a boy; she finally had her boy after two more girls.

My younger brother started to tease me. Mom did not have the tools or the no how to handle the situation with care. She always said, "Peter stop teasing your sister, Sarah, do not pay attention to him." I played into my brother's game as I enjoyed the attention. The teasing continued for years. After a while my brother started calling me stupid. Then one day, I came home from school, and he called me stupid again and I said, "Ok, I'm stupid." He stopped teasing me, but the damage had been done. The hurt went deep down in my core. It has taken a toll on self-esteem and years of inner work.

Growing up I keep everything inside for what I have say seems unimportant. I feel small. Back in September 1968, I have a convulsion that changes my life forever – a wakeup call, you might say. The medical diagnosis of this convulsion is low blood sugar or hypoglycemia. For every condition there is a spiritual side to that condition. An older male friend tells me to start writing, expressing what I am holding inside, and so begins the journey. Around this same time, I become interested in photography, through my father, who tells me I have a good eye.

I also start going to a new age church with the help of my best friend's mother. Spirit is guiding me, opening doors. I get introduced to a week long camp called California Interfaith Youthcamp. It is here that I receive the knowingness of the presence of God in everything.

I meet my future husband, Larry. We live together for 4 1/2 years. During this time, I am literally beating my head on the wall. I feel stupid fighting my inner demons. There is a lot anger. I hate myself. We get married Sept 1978 and 2 years later I become a mother. It was not easy but I managed. I continued to go the church I was introduced too. As our girls grew, I stopped using and he used more. He beat me, but I did not have the strength to move out. He would talk bad about me to our girls and then talk bad about our girls to me, causing much tension.

The minister at the Family Church of Marin passed away. I began the process of finding a new church as I needed that comfort, love and support to keep me going. I studied Sufism for a while, then one weekend I discovered a great church. This was the Marin Church of Religious Science. Here I started healing and working on myself even more. I take workshops, and classes. I go to a 5 day retreat called Women's Spirit. Here I peel away more layers of the onion. I am getting stronger in who I am.

I filled for divorce in Jan 2006. I heard a voice inside, loud and clear, "It's about time." I head back to work knowing

I got this. I move up to North Idaho after a trip to Bali. This is the best decision I make for myself, living on my own for the first time. I continue to write, grow and just be. I met my future husband Kevin.

Two years after I started writing, I got the idea to publish a book of my poems and photos. This idea becomes a vision that has sustained me all these years. Now some 44 years later it is manifest into reality.

The poems in this book tell the story of my life with all the pain, struggles and the growth I have created. It is broken into 3 parts.

- PART 1 GENESIS (1969 – 1979)

This is the beginning of the dance, where I write down my thoughts. Words come easily, as I struggle to find myself. I start to unleash some inner demons like anger, pain, feeling stupid, with low self-esteem and confidence. I am desperately seeking answers; writing often about a love I am looking for, finding much later in life.

- PART 2 EXODUS (1980 – 1996)

The middle road of the process, I am busy with life, being married and raising two daughters. I keep writing, mainly about life around me, striving to find the unique expression that I am. My dream, like most women is put on the back burner.

- PART 3 REVELATIONS (1997 – PRESENT)

Here in the last part of the journey I continue to evolve. I am growing more spiritually, healing my past and moving forward. My writing takes on deeper spiritual connections. Often the words just flow through me – a gift. The vision to get my work published resurfaces from the far reaches of my mind. A title is revealed to me, "Dancing With My Soul." My spirit continues to expand, becoming one with all that is.

Life is a dance with the divine, expressing fully each moment. In order to open up to this dance and live, we must become aware of the glorious beauty that exists everywhere around us. When we alive in nature, we bring joy into our hearts, allowing it to become the dance. We then embrace this dance through the indwelling presence that is, by our spiritual integrity, balance and harmony, becoming one with it.

*Photo above taken on the Wenatchee
River north of Leavenworth, Wash*

WATER IS LIFE
ALWAYS MOVING,
CONSTANTLY CHANGING

PART 1 – GENESIS
(1969-1979)

The Weed

The weed is here in front of me
Blowing with the wind, getting all knotted up.

This knotted weed is torn, broken, and slanted
By the increasing wind,
That gets stronger as the day wears on

But the new green grass, is here
To reach out its arms and capture the weed,
That is dead, dry, and worthless.

I am the weed,
That is soaring with the endless wind.

A Straw In The Wind

A straw in the wind, is sailing through a storm,
Like the seagulls that do the same
For the face is bewildered and slightly lopsided.
The hair is put behind the ears
And the mouth is wide open.
A nose is pointed
And the man is astonished
To see this straw in the wind disappear
Into the vast fullness that beholds the sky.

Photo taken on the Mickinrick Trail, Sandpoint, ID

Wind Felt

Feeling the gentle winds beat upon my brow so strong
Bringing the warmth, they convey into my heart once more

How was I to know that it was just a freedom? Ready to catch
me in its loving arms

A Light

The earth and sky were dark, as dark as could be, when off
in the horizon a light was seen by the sun, that was setting
behind the clouds and allowed us to see the world. This light
let off a path down the ocean.

I was totally amazed; it was so beautiful.

Found

You walk home under the flowery sun,
That sends down sweltering rays.
Your eyes are dazed, and your head is whirling.
You are lost in a story – book of wonder,
Opening its doors to a musical sound,
And the honeyed stupendous vibrating
From the warm molded hills,
Rolling on to invisible sight

A Spot Of Sun

A spot of sun is all my own
Jumping, escaping in the slow faint breeze
With natures music playing upon my ears
I feel the sun shining bright as it can be.

Photo taken on Gold Creel, Sandpoint, ID

Look Into Your Eyes

As I look into your eyes,I see a bird soaring freely
I see the hills aflame with color swaying in the breeze

A white hollow vision is hovering above
Infinite in size and shape yet vivid
As it seems it is me

It makes you lively on your toes step high and be
For I see a new dimension as I look into your eyes

Seasons

The weather is warm, and the kids start school
The leaves do change with autumn about

The rain falls and the leaves wither and die
The sea rumbles, when winter rolls along

Spring is heaven, when flowers are blooming,
And the birds are singing with the green growing

The people gather on the shores of the deep blue ocean,
And travel to many lands when summer arrives

A New Day

Radiance dim and yellow,
Seen on the early morn
Shimmering through the green woods
Like the delightful sounds so harsh.
Crested kingfishers alive
Blue eagle of darkest hue
Trolley car shrill and slow
Imperative penetrating bell
Deafening the weary ear
With water splashing and dashing
Over the purple poisonous berries
And curved dense forests
Surrounding the bare landscape

Driftwood

Driftwood sits on the beach,
Lying on the cold wet sand
After being washed in by the sea, from a storm
A blank man looks like a dog.
His nose is long and droopy
His body all separated from the soul
And the eyes look forward
Producing a tear of fright
Exploring the reaches beyond mankind
For driftwood is seen again.

And now a whale with an eye looking,
A tooth bold and bright,
A woman standing tall deformed yet beautiful
Become the driftwood sitting on the beach again

Pearls

O, sea of pearls on the ocean floor,
O, little smile of joy that is so bright.
A shell crying
To a large rock
A shell sleeping
To an elegant tone
Rasp for the gentle touch, woman of the pearl
Out of the little smile joy,
That is bright
Rasp for just one pearl.

Photo taken in Bali, Indonesia

The Plum Blossom

I picked a white plum blossom
From her green leafed tree
Oh, you should have seen the blossom there

And the rain fell from the treacherous sky
To see the shrunken difference there

I spun around to the plum blossom
That turned you into a dream
The beautiful dream of love

There you will stay,
Along with the roaring waves
Like the ways of the sea

Untitled

Weakly she laughed in the lofty sun,
While the angle upon her brow doth shone,
Like puzzled mice on an aged bun
Who kept closed a microscopic tone?\
As tarnished, she sits in oval bone.
But soon his eyes shrunk to a size untold
For his lady's purpose was honeyed to the fold
Tears, at the thought of those enchantments old,
And Madeline snoring in the lap of shelter cold

The Puppet

A puppet sits in a dim dark closet, is seen at midnight and is talked about by those who are high.

The puppet is put on sticks, with long dangling strings that make him move, where he is seen moving by the high people. He speaks to them of a few unimportant words.

Then the puppet is dying, laying on the cold closet floor, from overusing his muscles, which are very weak and molded.

Photo taken at South Beach State Park, Newport Oregon

Dark Dreams

The dark dream is here
And here it stays, for today wonder is seen,
Wonder that flows in and out and out and in.

The dark dream has fallen
To the deep ocean, where it becomes haunted
A young man comes up to me
And says, "You shall be seen no more"

For the young man picked me up
And threw me far below in the ocean.
Cur-splash I went.

I soon became haunted because the dark dreams are…
And there I was not able to get back to life.

Wanted

Put your hand in your pocket m' friend and feel the sparking, flavorful, distinctive painting that made a marriage legal.

Gripped by emotion you jump into a different breed of cat that recreates the era of manly elegance.

Fall in love if you will, but please let's not be irresponsible about it for a diamond is forever and an instant loading is the beginning.

But there are others who need help not only yourself.
Wanted ... someone to love us.

The Bird

The bird who flies high and low, is trapped beneath the waves, which come rolling in endlessly making a hollow sound and splashing over the rocks.

This bird becomes helpless, for his wings are too wet to fly. He is eventually washed up on the dead and endless shore.

A person is seen walking by, he stops and looks at the bird, who is sitting, waiting for help, the waves splashing over him. The person picks up the bird by the beak and throws him around.

The tide is going out and this poor little bird is all dry, but his left wing is broken from being tossed around.

When the tide came back in, the bird is washed back, to the large ocean, where he died soon afterwards and sank to the lifeless bottom.

Photo taken just north of Depot Bay on the Oregon coast

The Kiss

A kiss soft and gentle, as it flows through the earth
Touches those in need, with
Eyes folded, ears caught
Lips pressed against mine
A light shines, and I sing

Pitter Patter

The rain that goes pitter patter on the window pane, Sounds
like the bullets that pitter patter against the chest of the soul.

The Peace March

It was a cold November Saturday, that 200,000+ people
descended upon San Francisco and marched for peace

In that crowd many people got lost lonely and desperate
to find someone they knew

We gathered at the Polo Fields, where it was jammed packed
with cold hungry people

At 3:00 in the afternoon, there were many still streaming in
Bon fires were built, to keep warm and burn the trash piles

But this was not allowed, police came in and made a fuss
People started dancing in circles

At 5:00 when the rally was over, a person was seen holding a
sign that said " Colorado"

My Bedroom

I have a little bedroom, that is a wonderful sight
You look out the window, into the glazing light
The curtains are open, the people stare,
I lie on my bed looking at those who glare.
I sit; just sit thinking, playing the guitar,
And writing many things, like the North Star

Photo was taken at Cascade Creek in Mill Valley, CA

Green Leaves Say Hello

The green swaying leaves say hello
When you stare up at them
And look into their lives

They make a soft, sweet relaxing sound,
That bends and falls with the gentle breeze
And sings into your ears

The glistening setting sun shines on them
Like diamonds on the sea
And yet they are not to be touched

For the leaves that are green turn brown
Starting fresh next spring

Thoughts

You listen to the pungent words,
Sailing through the air, with a silvery flash of a tail,
Acting like a daisy on the foot

I have a little lover that follows me around.
This lover is that of God
For he is one that makes things grow and be.

You sit by the beaming sun,
That is soaring up, behind the first raindrops.
Ashy, brown mountains tarnish in the fields beyond.
Colors cook with the wind.

Photo taken from the top of Multnomah Falls

PART 2 – EXODUS
(1980–1996)

A Safe Space

Growing up my small bedroom and beach below Become my
refuge as I strive
To find peace in the dysfunction surrounding me

The bedroom sits on the downstairs front corner
Of that old summer cottage
Renovated into a beautiful two-story house
Windows address the front and sides

A short narrow bookcase stands next to the door
Moving to the right a cedar lined closet
Against the wall is a heater
With a chest of drawers nearby

The bed is just a box spring and mattress
With a pile of sand under the covers at the foot
A simple desk and high back woven chair
Occupy the rest of the space
The beach named Muir Beach is the gateway of
Redwood Creek
As it wines its way to the Pacific Ocean
Sand dunes sit at the end like gumdrops

Beyond that the rolling hills go on
Beaches, rocks, cliffs and coves make up the coastline
As they find their way to the Golden Gate.

I spend hours lying on my bed or sitting at the desk Listening
and watching, the people, creek, beach, and waves

Change from season to season for nineteen years Creating a
safe space

Photo taken at Muir Beach, Marin County, CA

Crossing A Mid-Winter Creek At The Beach

A flat beach and stagnant lagoo
Change after the first rains,
As the creek breaks away to the ocean
Water cuts into the sand,
Forming banks that grow

One mid-winter morning I awake
And see this enormous sand bank
Dressing the opposite shore
Excited, I grab a coat and run – Barefoot.

The bitter cold water,
Like crystals, tickles my purple feet.
Should I go on or turn around
The immense slope stretches before me.
I cringe as pebbles jab my tender toes.

Sand keeps falling around me,
As I struggle up the embankment, to no avail.
Spying an easier spot downstream,
I climb up and begin pushing
The beach down the steep slop,
Trying not to slip,
Watching the sand plunge, with a splash
And disappear forever.

Pinecrest Lake

My dancing room is alive.

A path winding around this deep rich blue lake
Nestled between tall Digger pines and huge granite rock

Opens my heart to the grandeur set before me.

Sparkles of sunlight dance on the water's surface
Quiet coves hug the shore
Boulders sandwiched one on another
Trees growing out of cracks
People playing on the distant sandy beach like busy ants
I stroll on and ponder.
A small green meadow opens up to tall sparse grass.
Curved walls of granite
Slide into a fast-moving bubby creek,
While juts of pillars stand on the opposite side
And a sturdy wooden bridge crosses.

The path climbs high above the lake
Huge boulders reach the water edge.
Realizing time is running short
I quickly press on, knowing that for now
My dancing room is gone
Allowing me to return again and again

A Vision

I am sitting on a rich green meadow by a stream
Colorful flowers dance in the fresh early morning breeze
The stream is crystal clear, singing gently, flowing
And churning over the many-hued stones
The sun's rays begin to play with the objects like diamonds
I stand on top of a mountain and see the glory before me
I am filled and smile.

Photo taken at Copper Creek near the
Canadian Border in Idaho

Blackstone Canyon

Stepping onto this open space,
We feel a strong sense of peace,
With Spirit kissing the face
Listening to the joyful rushing creek,
Sing its way toward the bay.
We sit on a moss-covered rock,
And embrace a moment of no time
While water cascades down the hillside
Into a small stream that winds its way to the creek.
Ferns cling to the banks,
Dancing in the soft breeze
A spot of sunlight peaks through the trees,
And a soft rain falls.
A waterfall thunders into a deep pool
More water drips from the rich green moss.
Dabbled sunlight makes a strong presence on the hillside
I feel your presence here,
Knowing the beauty that surrounds me,
Is ever singing in my soul

Touching The Inner Core

For just one short week, the mountains become a retreat
Where a group of us gather together and live

I come torn, lost, unsure, sharing myself
Searching, listening, and receiving answers
Wanting to be free of the addictions plaguing my life

Can I have one those massages?
I ask a wise, powerful, dear, spiritual woman
Yes, you are finally ready, and so it begins:
Deep Breakfast by Ray Lynch plays softy
Echoing through the tall pine trees
She invites me to climb onto the table,
Lie on my back, get comfortable and close my eyes
Reaching deep into my subconscious
She begins whispering words into my right ear
Your smoking grass no longer serves you
It is not who you are; you are better then that
Her hands gently stroke my stomach
Allowing the old habits to disappear and fall away.
I feel empty, drained.

Then the reading continues,
I embrace new ways of being

The hands move up my torso, to the shoulders, neck and face
They gently caress my head which becomes as light as feather
My ears catch some powerful words I am God. I AM GOD.
The voice stops.
I slowly open my eyes, blinking a couple of times
Tears flow freely and easily
I find myself hovering above, floating with the clouds

My heart is full, my mind clear,
I am glowing, filled with love
After a light dinner, I reach out to a male friend
Where a shared past experience, of holding hands
And being awake all night
Evokes a warm closeness, growing into an aching feeling

Every cell alive
He puts his arms around me
And for two minutes we are as One
We part; his lips lightly touch mine

Later that same evening in song circle
I feel the words to the song The Rose
Penetrate my innermost core, tears flow.

Poetry

Poetry is a plow that turns up time
It is a way of seeing things, not saying things
Poetry is the music that sings in our souls
Waiting to be expressed
It is everywhere
      The way water flows
      The song of the birds
      The whisper of the grass
      The silence of a forest
      And the colors of life
Poetry is reaching beyond the obvious going deeper

Photo taken in Bali, Indonesia

Heckel

We cared for him
A Sulfur Crested Cockatoo

Hand raised from infancy
He was an extraordinary bird.

He danced from side to side
One foot up, then the other
Turning his head around
He swung upside down
On your finger and inside his cage

Perched on a shoulder
A gentle touch to the cheek
With kisses and clicks
Black beady eyes always looking

His down, like velvet
Was in constant need of
Being scratched and rubbed
His head would turn with delight.
A lifted claw on your hand was
"More, don't stop, more."

When excited or scared
His yellow crest rose
Loud squawks heard
Hopping up and down
He was home outdoors
With a full set of wings
He took off flying higher and higher
"I'm free. I'm free.

Yes, he was much loved
The character that he was

The Virgin Delight Of Autumn

Sitting next to the creek,
On the exposed river rock,
We embrace the virgin delight of autumn,
Kissing our beings

We see shadows dancing with the sunlight,
On the water's surface
The peaceful creek flows along
Rippling through the rocks
Hugging the shore

Green grasses and ferns play
An Aspen from one trunk splits
Becoming two, entwined yet still one

Red, yellow, brown, green, and orange leaves float past,
On their way home
Rising in love, we sing
Embracing this virgin dance of autumn

Photo taken in Bali, Indonesia

An English Sunset

The evening train rumbling fast to Harwich,
To catch the night ferry
I look up and see,
An orange, zigzag line,
Race across the evening sky,
Acting like a streak of lightning,
Becoming a mountain range
Above dark clouds
In the middle, the setting sun
Reveals a flaming ball of fire, red and orange
It is a glimpse of twilight,
That takes me home for a moment.

PART 3 – REVELATIONS
(1997–present)

A Dance With Life

Let me take you on a Journey
A dance with life begins.
From within, a light shines forth,
Shields fall away, doors open.
I become one with All that is,
A yearning to reach out, touch and grow
I embrace this dance of life as Love.
An orange sunrise on the horizon
Flowers blooming in a field of green
Yellow, blue, purple, and red dots come alive.
A waterfall thundering, down a rock face
A stream gently babbling along
A mighty oak stands majestically, in a golden field.
Clouds dance with the winds ever changing.
The constant hum of the ocean,
With waves breaking on a sandy shore
A momma duck, with her babies
Swimming in the reeds
The first dusting of snow in the high mountains
And a red sunset at dusk
All bring peace, awe, beauty, and gratitude to my soul
Showing me the richness of God
A dance with life is radiant.
Anchored in this knowingness
I am one with the dance of life,

An infinite symphony, playing in harmony
The one song – one essence
Of love and light
With joyful music flowing from my heart, I sing.
I absolutely see this dance with life
Is the magic of God, All in All Now.
Embrace it, live it, feel it, be the dance.

Being Alive

Rain fell from the sky,
Drenching the land for days,
When one day the sun came out,
I took to walking up Black Stone Canyon.

The creek full, singing and dancing,
Water everywhere,
Oozing out of the earth,
Streaming down the hillsides,
Like ribbons, flowing

Walking further down the canyon
Darkness closed in, penetrating my core
And then I heard it,
Distant, yet present
The waterfall, thundering,
Her arms outstretched like silken threads.
Beckoning me to sit beside her

The Healing Earth

Shadows falling
Light enhancing
Love unfolding
Emerging as One
We live in Peace

Photo taken on the Cascade Trail,
Mt Tamalpais State Park, Marin County, CA

Laughter

Laughter is the song of the soul
It opens us up to a greater Joy.
And warms our hearts,
It allows the stresses of the day to dissolve.
Laugh more each day, a deep belly laugh
Let your heart sing with its Joy.
Be brighten by the laughter of others,
Feel their warmth,
Spreading like a wave.
Capture it.
Drink it.
Fill your vessel with it.
Life is good. Laugh more.

A Dance With Some Faries

I step outside at work
Only to be greeted
By a cluster of leaves
Moving into a dance
They form a circle
Twirling around in the breeze

Taking my hand
They invite me to join them
In this dance
I am filled with joy and delight
Being reminded
Of the little pleasures
I receive in life.

I smile and say
Thank you for this gift today

Photo taken on the Mickinnick trail, Sandpoint, Id

To My Mother, The Picnic

After your passing, we gathered together,
All four of us, your children,
And headed for Deadmans Bluff
High above the American River east of Auburn,
With sandwiches and plenty of other food in tow,
For a quiet, reflective picnic

Sitting in this stillness
We smell the sweet scent of pine
Enhancing our beings
A whisper of a breeze, softly caress the ears.
Sunlight dances with leaves
We feel your presence here,
Singing through the tall trees
We are at peace,
Embracing the love and beauty that surrounds us

My Dearest Little Sarah

A child of God stands before me.
I welcome you with open arms.
A beautiful precious baby
So innocent and pure, a light to behold
You are special, as magic sings in the air.
Cute as a button, a smile waits

I am here for you.
I care for you and love you.
I will help you to be strong,
To stand up for yourself and keep control
I will help you hold on to your own power,
And not let go

Let us grow together,
Play and keep that innocence.
It is wonderful to see you smile again.
Let me light a path for you to follow,
As we let the love of God shine forth in our lives
I honor and value you, as a little girl and as a woman.
I love you with all my heart
And send you a big hug and a kiss.

Love Always, Sarah

A Sensuous Side

She stands by the window, in the early morning light
With a flowing white gown on
Waiting
The sun shining on her golden hair
Her full breasts, soft as velvet
Exposed
She yearned for him, a warm embrace
Followed by a passionate kiss
Becoming one
Still waiting

A Sheet Of Glass

Riding a night train from Belgium to Innsbruck, Austria
I awake at the crack of dawn,
To find myself coming out of a tunnel
Glazing my eyes upon a most breath-taking sight
An opaque mountain lake
As still as a sheet of glass, not a ripple, total peace
A rich green meadow lined the front and right side
Off to the left stand high snow-covered peaks,
While in the distance a waterfall flows
As I drink in the beauty, my heart opens up
And I feel a great sense of gratitude

The Present Is Pregnant
With Possibilities

I open the sliding glass door
And listen. Listen
To the creek rushing past
The snow falling, swirling silent
Crystals forming each flake different - ice
The wind whispering through the trees
I listen to the grandness of life now
The past is history; the future is the magic unfolding
And the present is a gift waiting to be opened
Pregnant with possibilities

Photo taken at Rattlesnake Creek, Missoula, MT

The Heartbeat Of The Mother

The pulsating beat of the scared drum
Opens my eyes and heart
To the organic rocks growing
Out from the banks of the river

Lines and curves come alive
Appearing as gods, goddess, hearts, and creatures
Of the land, exposing their wonder
They reach out and sing to me
As I yearn to touch them
Being drawn into their world

In the eye of the stillness and silence
The heartbeat of that scared drum
Is a beautiful song playing the one note.
Connecting me to the mother

Photo taken on Mickinnick Trail, Sandpoint, ID

A Touch Of Green
In The Creek

Water flows into a pool,
Easing with the currents
Over submerged rocks

A tiny, green leaf, is a cross
Perfect form, perfect symmetry
Becoming one
With a brown, moss-covered rock.

I am this leaf
Perfect form, perfect body
One

Now a pine needle attaches itself
To this touch of green in the creek
Becoming one with it
Dancing
Embracing
The One I Am.

Passion

Passion is the fire of the Soul,
An intense, inner, driving force,
An overwhelming feeling or conviction
The color red, a rose, bleeding
Passion loves what we do
Pursing our dreams
And embracing the success we achieve
Passion is good for the soul
Expanding the richness in our lives to greater depth
Passion is being in love with life
In all its wonder and glory – Alive
Sitting by a body of water
Being an inspiration, creating magic each moment
And enjoying a quiet interlude

An Opening In My Heart

I glow in the softness of the connection in my heart,
An innocence opening to the divine mother,
Resonating deep within me
A tender touch, a warm embrace, sweet words,
A beautiful smile, glazing into your eyes, seeing the soul
Asking me to let go and just be in the moment.
I feel tender, vulnerable and love at the same time
I am the divine mother, embracing my femininity.
And experiencing a profound joy,
As I open my heart in this space

A Timeless Moment

Streak of sunlight across
A brown fast-moving creek
Smiles upon my brow

Photo taken at Silver Creek Falls State Park, OR

This Moment Now

We stand on edge of time waiting.
Waiting
For that precise moment to flitter past
And yet if we just open our eyes
We can see the magnificence around us
Falling into that moment
Fading into another moment
Even more grandeur than before
Always looking ahead
Staying present, the moment before us is Now

Transformation

Small iridescent blue butterflies
Cross my path again
Creating newness, healing

Flow

A creek is music in motion, flowing gently along
Dancing and gurgling in an endless weaving path
Cascading over rocks and singing off cliffs
Peace and harmony fill my aching soul
As I am struck by the awesome beauty
Everywhere around me

My Little Lover

I have a little lover that follows me around,
This lover is that of God,
For he is the one who makes things grow and be.

Nearer than hands and feet,
My little lover is the all Knowing presence,
The pulsating energy, the heart beat,
Dwelling within all life everywhere.
It is the great I AM.

Photo taken from the bridge at Multnomah Falls, Oregon

A Humming Echos The Land

Dancing on the edge of my dreams,
I reach out and touch you,
Pulling you into me
I feel your warm embrace holding me close.
And yet, as I look at your magnificence
I can hear it, a humming,
The universal Om
Penetrating deep into the core,
Vibrating like a womb impregnated,
Giving birth to new ideas,
Growing beyond the visible, encircling the globe

You sing your song to me, As I sit here in the quiet
Through the whisper in the tall trees,
A woodpecker enjoying a tasty meal, birds singing,
A clap of thunder rolling through the afternoon sky,
And a gentle rain soaking the ground
You are here with me enriching my soul.
Vibrant colors come alive,
As greens of growing intensity shoot up,
After a blanket of white melts
I can feel it, in the very essence
Of all that is, going deeper
This humming energy exploding, expanding

Echoing throughout the land,
Reaching a wonderful peaceful place within
The Om rests here.
I shout for joy. Happiness envelopes me,
As love sinks in, seeing this beauty spring forth, before me
Returning me to the Divine that I am

A Helping Hand

Life is a gift with all the problems, challenges to help us grow and become stronger.

We talk to God and give him all our conditions as gifts, he can then open them up and with a helping hand can heal the situation. We feel lighter and free, when we let God take over and sprinkle gold dust on life.

Photo taken at Big Creek, Montana

Creating Our Happy And Allowing Magic To Unfold

We create our happy when we step outside the box and play
Saying YES to everything, the good and the bad
We celebrate life and breathe in
The awesome beauty surrounding us
In silence we can go to a heart space,
Experience mindfulness, listen, forgive, and be grateful,
We see the lesson being taught.
And ask to have the blocks removed, that hold us back
We begin to see more clearly,
Surrendering to the glory that resides within – the I AM
We watch what we say, think and do,
As our feelings come from our thoughts,
That manifest into reality
Allowing life to unfold with grace
We create our magic each step of the way
Our happy lives and we are lifted,
As we connect with one another in love
Changing our story and thriving
Saying YES to all of life

The Mountains Call To Me

I hike a well-used trail,
Through meadows and rock outcroppings
Spring is alive here,
As wildflowers of all kinds
Show off their exquisite beauty
In an array of pinks, oranges, yellows, blues, reds and whites

Climbing higher, I reach Round Lake
It sings to me. I dive in.
The cold penetrates every cell of my being.
I am one. Refreshed
Majestic mountain peaks surround me,
As rich greens and blues intensify, in their magnitude

Quacking Aspens dance in the breeze,
Pines whisper back.
I am touched deep in my soul.
The Feather River meanders its way past.
A soft rippling caresses my heart.

A frequent train chugs past.
Cars wising by and sounds of laughter

Take me away, for just a moment
From this place of connectedness

Birds sing their song of love and joy
And I return once again to the peace and harmony
Of river, the creek, and the mountains
Calling to me

Standing Behind The Falls

Walking down the winding path
We stand behind the falls
Feeling the spray upon our face
A wall of water in front of us
Thundering off the cliff above
While far below a rainbow forms
Time passes as we slip into nothingness
And evolve into no time seeing beyond the visible
Feeling the awesome power of love flowing
A crack opens to let the light in

Photo taken at Silver Creek Falls State Park, OR

In The Silence

In the silence there is stillness.
In the stillness, Peace exists.
The sounds, smells
What we see, hear and feel come alive GOD
As we live in this silence,
We dwell in the present moment NOW.

Photo taken at Starvation Creek Falls, Oregon

The Path Of I Am

It is at a weekend sufi retreat, where I experience the profound, power of the great I am, presence. We assemble on a knoll, where our leader helps us gather our energy. We circle clockwise then counter-clockwise, chanting. We descend down the hill in silence and begin to walk through the land. I feel light headed and connected with all that is. I AM.

A narrow overgrown path with many shades of green We stop, our leader goes to the back and sends three young men home for talking. I am right up front in awe. The leaves shimmering, alive, with splashes of vivid colors, become a dance. I AM.

A small stream, flowing down hill. I desire to float across but I catch myself thinking No. I AM.

Soon a waterfall thunders down a granite face, where Moss and fern hang on, dripping into a clear blue pool below.
I AM.

An opening of light presses itself against me,
Flows through me,
Exposing a sloping meadow dotted with bits of yellow.
I AM.

Tall trees caress my soul, while a small deep lake,
Rests on top of large boulders, like a sheet of glass,
Not a ripple, total peace. I AM.

I sit and ponder, looking up at the clouds,
Listening to the birds echoing in my ears,
How grand and abundant God is,
Knowing what God is, I AM.

As Old As Time

There is a place, in northern California as old as time, where one can go, to recharge the body, revitalize the mind, rejuvenate the spirit and fill the heart with gratitude, existing from a deep seeded memory. It is the primeval forest.

As I walk into Stout Grove in Jediahua Smith State Park, I feel alive, my senses awake. A path going down, and winding around and through these old growth redwood trees is well worn and rich with wonder. The air fragrant, the environment clean and pristine.

Deep green lichens cling to the trees while Spanish moss drips from the branches. A fallen tree brings new life into the picture, creating knots, hollows and smooth stumps that form characters. The undergrowth is thick and lush. Birds singing everywhere, the Smith River silently flows past far below, while ripples of water dance with me.

The bark is red, rough and furry, and their grits are massive. Their heights impressive, soaring to a canopy high above, where filtered sunlight shines through this magical very old forest. Alder trees also live in this special place.

It is a powerful journey one can take again and again full of energy and life.

My Life As A Carrot

I could be a pea, a bean, a beet, a squash,
Or any other kind of vegetable for that matter
But today I'm a carrot.
I sit in a package with my brothers and sisters
Waiting to be picked up off the shelf
Then one bright spring day, it happens
And I'm in a bag with several other seed packs
Ready to be taken to my new home
My package gets cut open and I'm poured out
Among all my family members and planted
We are close together, kissing each other
But I'm scattered out – Ah yes, a little more room.
I'm tucked in and watered.
My parents care for me, so I surprise them
Being the first to come up
A tiny sprout, then more feathery leaves burst out.
My roots get stronger, and
I dig myself deeper, into the rich, soil
Earthworms stop by and say Hello
I grow more, getting bigger, longer and
Turning a vibrant orange
Then finally my top is exposed and I'm ready
My brothers and sisters have followed suite
And a bunch of us are pulled, cleaned, cut up,
Put into a pot and cooked

Twenty minutes later we are daubed with salt
And butter and eaten
Our parents tell us over and over
We are so good, sweet and delicious
A smile comes across my face, as I settle inside.

Sarah Catherine Smith was born on June 21,1951. She grew up in Muir Beach, CA. She received an AS degree in photography at College of Marin. She started writing her thoughts down in 1969. She has taken trips to Bali, the Pacific Northwest and California. She now lives in Idaho, where she continues to write, work and create. This is her first book.

www.ingramcontent.com/pod-product-compliance
Lightning Source LLC
Chambersburg PA
CBHW051228120626
46547CB00013B/1559

*9 7 9 8 8 9 6 3 3 0 0 2 8 *